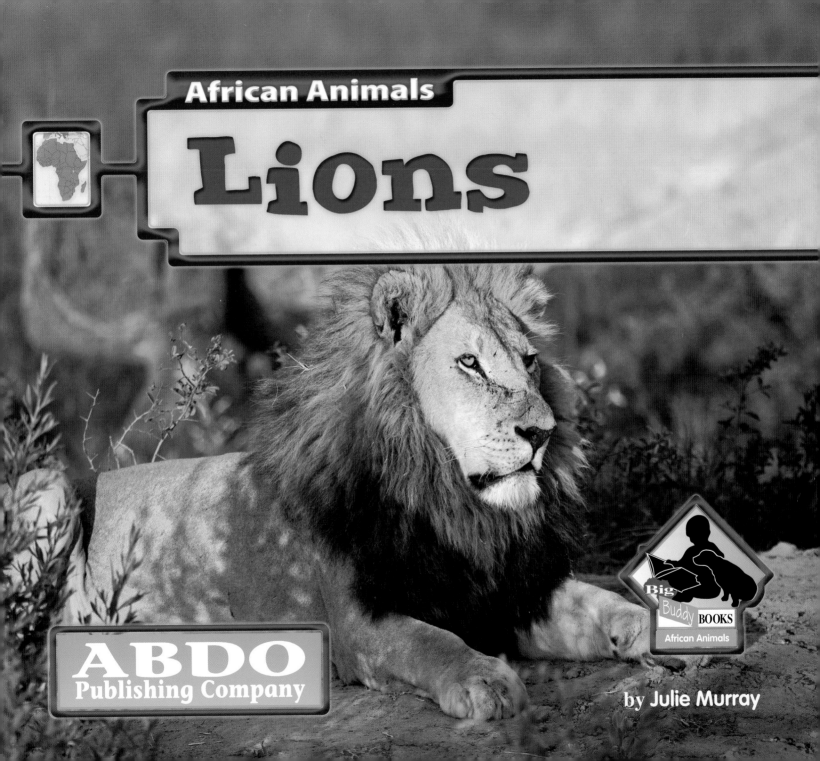

African Animals

Lions

ABDO
Publishing Company

Big Buddy BOOKS
African Animals

by Julie Murray

VISIT US AT
www.abdopublishing.com

Published by ABDO Publishing Company, PO Box 398166, Minneapolis, MN 55439.

Printed in the United States of America, North Mankato, Minnesota.
102011
012012

♻ PRINTED ON RECYCLED PAPER

Coordinating Series Editor: Rochelle Baltzer
Editor: Marcia Zappa
Contributing Editors: Megan M. Gunderson, BreAnn Rumsch, Sarah Tieck
Graphic Design: Maria Hosley
Cover Photograph: *iStockphoto*: ©iStockphoto.com/pjmalsbury.
Interior Photographs/Illustrations: *Corbis* (pp. 5, 23); *iStockphoto*: ©iStockphoto.com/brytta (p. 4), ©iStockphoto.com/Essence (p. 8), ©iStockphoto.com/princessdlaf (p. 9), ©iStockphoto.com/PTB-images (p. 4); *Photolibrary*: Age fotostock (p. 25), Bios (p. 15), Imagebroker.net (p. 27), Monsoon Images (p. 23), Goldstein Paul (p. 19), Peter Arnold Images (pp. 9, 21, 27); *Shutterstock*: Bersanelli (p. 11), clickit (p. 10), Ivan Kuzmin (p. 23), Jin Young Lee (p. 12), Alta Oosthuizen (p. 7), Jakub Pavlinec (p. 9), Patrick Poendl (p. 8), Dave Pusey (p. 29), Graeme Shannon (p. 13), Wild At Art (p. 15), Oleg Znamenskiy (p. 17).

Library of Congress Cataloging-in-Publication Data

Murray, Julie, 1969-
  Lions / Julie Murray.
     p. cm. -- (African animals)
  ISBN 978-1-61783-221-5
  1. Lion--Juvenile literature. I. Title.
  QL737.C23M895 2012
  599.757--dc23
                              2011028955

Contents

Amazing African Animals 4

Lion Territory 6

Jambo! Welcome to Africa! 8

Take a Closer Look 10

Pride Life 14

New Men 18

Great Hunters 20

Baby Lions 24

Survivors 28

Masalala! I'll bet you never knew… 30

Important Words 31

Web Sites 31

Index 32

Long ago, nearly all land on Earth was one big mass. About 200 million years ago, the land began to break into **continents**. One of these is Africa.

In the wild, lions are only found in Africa and a small area of India.

Africa is the second-largest **continent**. It is known for hot weather, wild land, and interesting animals. One of these animals is the lion. The lion is often called "king of the beasts" for its power and strength.

Lion Territory

Most lions live in the eastern and southern parts of central Africa. They are found in grasslands, **savannas**, and open woodlands.

SAHARA DESERT

Nile River

▨ Lion Territory

Tall grass helps lions hide while hunting.

Jambo! Welcome to Africa!

If you took a trip to where lions live, you might find…

…many languages.

More than 1,000 languages are spoken across Africa! Swahili (swah-HEE-lee) is common in central and eastern Africa where lions live. In Swahili, *jambo* is a greeting for visitors. *Masalala* means "goodness!" or "wow!" And *simba* means "lion."

…the Sahara Desert.

The Sahara Desert is the largest desert in the world. It is about the same size as the United States!

...cassavas and plantains.

African farmers grow different crops from those grown in the United States. Cassavas (*left*) are common vegetables. They are similar to potatoes. Plantains (*below*) are similar to bananas. They can be fried, baked, or grilled.

...safaris.

A safari is a special trip to see African animals in the wild. Safaris last a few days to several weeks. They bring people up close to animals such as lions, elephants, leopards, and rhinoceroses.

Take a Closer Look

Lions are members of the cat family. They have thick, **muscular** bodies. Their large heads have big mouths and noses and small, round ears.

Lions have gold or brownish fur. An adult male lion also has a mane. This long, thick circle of hair often surrounds his face and neck. It makes him look even bigger and stronger than he is. And, it guards his neck during fights.

A lion's mane may include gold, reddish, brown, or black hair. It gets darker as he grows older.

A young male starts to grow his mane when he is about one year old. His mane is fully grown around five years.

Male lions are larger than females. Adult males are about four feet (1.2 m) tall at their shoulders. They are usually more than nine feet (2.7 m) long with their tails stretched out. Adult male lions weigh 330 to 550 pounds (150 to 250 kg).

Lions are the second-largest animals in the cat family. Only tigers are larger.

Pride Life

Most lions live in groups called prides. Prides usually have 10 to 20 members. But some have up to 40! Each pride has a few males, several females, and their young.

Members of a pride usually get along well. They often purr, lick each other, and rub cheeks and heads.

Every lion pride has its own territory. This can be as large as 100 square miles (260 sq km)! But when food and water are plentiful, this area is usually much smaller.

Lions do not allow other predators to hunt in their territory. They warn others to stay away by marking the area with their scent. If a predator enters a pride's territory, the males roar and chase it away.

Uncovered!

Lions rest and sleep about 20 hours a day. They are most active during the cool, dark hours of night.

Lions are the only cats that live in groups.

New Men

Female lions, or lionesses, stay in the same pride their whole lives. Young males leave the pride when they are two to four years old. Then, they wander in small groups. Usually the groups are made up of brothers or male cousins.

From time to time, a group of wandering males **challenges** the males in a pride. If they beat them in a fight, they take over the pride and its territory.

New males take over a pride every two to three years.

19

Great Hunters

Lions are **carnivores**. They eat large animals including wildebeests, zebras, giraffes, buffalo, rhinoceroses, and hippopotamuses.

Lionesses do most of the hunting. They often hunt in groups. This allows them to catch **prey** that are bigger and faster than they are.

Lionesses are sneaky hunters. Several of them creep behind their prey and hide. Then, another lioness chases the prey toward the waiting hunters.

Lions are built to hunt. They can see, hear, and smell well. They have very strong front legs. And their front paws have sharp, curved claws to hold prey.

Uncovered!

When a lion isn't using its claws, it can pull them into its paws. This keeps the claws sharp!

After a successful hunt, lions eat as much as they can. All the lions in a pride eat together. But, they do not share the catch equally. Males get the most, followed by lionesses and then young lions.

Lions are not picky eaters. When there is not enough large **prey**, they hunt smaller animals. This includes hares and birds. Lions may also **scavenge** dead animals. And, they even steal prey from cheetahs and hyenas.

Uncovered!
Wandering male lions hunt for themselves or scavenge dead animals.

An adult male lion can eat up to 75 pounds (34 kg) of meat in one meal! But, he usually only eats about 15 pounds (7 kg).

Lions have 30 sharp teeth. But, they do not chew their food. Instead, they tear it up and swallow it in chunks.

Lions eat what they catch right away. After a big catch, they may not hunt again for a few days.

Baby Lions

Lions are **mammals**. Female lions have one to six babies at a time. Baby lions are called cubs. At birth, they weigh two to four pounds (1 to 2 kg). Newborn lion cubs are blind and helpless.

Lion cubs risk being hunted by hyenas, leopards, and other predators. So, their mother moves them to a new spot every few days. She chooses spots well hidden in tall grass.

Uncovered!
Males want only their own cubs to live in their pride. So when new males take over a pride, they often kill all the cubs.

A lioness gently carries her cubs in her mouth.

Often, several females in a pride give birth around the same time. So, cubs can drink milk from any of the mothers.

At first, lion cubs drink their mother's milk. After one and a half to three months, cubs begin to eat meat. They eat their mother's **prey**.

Around 11 to 18 months, cubs start learning how to hunt. They stay with their mother until they can hunt on their own. Usually, this happens when cubs are about 20 to 30 months old.

Uncovered!
Lions are full grown after five to six years.

Cubs are often playful. They chase each other and pretend to fight.

Survivors

Life in Africa isn't easy for lions. New buildings and farms take over their **habitats**. **Prey** is not as common as it once was. And, some people kill lions. They do this to keep farm animals safe or to show bravery.

Still, lions **survive**. Farmers are learning how to keep their animals safe without killing lions. And, there are laws against hunting lions that live in certain areas. Lions help make Africa an amazing place.

Uncovered!

Lions in Africa are vulnerable. This means they are in some danger of dying out. Lions in India are endangered. This means they are in great danger of dying out. Scientists believe there are only about 350 lions left in India.

In the wild, lions live 10 to 15 years.

Masalala!

I'll bet you never knew...

...that a lion's roar is so loud it can be heard five miles (8 km) away!

...that lion cubs are easy to train. Lions are very smart! When trainers start working with cubs at an early age, cubs can learn many tricks. This makes lions popular in circuses and other shows. But, even trained lions are still wild animals. So, people working with them are never completely safe.

...that lions and tigers have had babies together! Their cubs are called tigons or ligers. These cubs have only been born in zoos and animal parks, not in the wild.

30

Important Words

carnivore an animal or a plant that eats meat.

challenge (CHA-luhnj) to test one's strength or abilities.

continent one of Earth's seven main land areas.

habitat a place where a living thing is naturally found.

mammal a member of a group of living beings. Mammals make milk to feed their babies and usually have hair or fur on their skin.

muscular (MUHS-kyuh-luhr) having strong, well-developed muscles. Muscles are body tissues, or layers of cells, that help the body move.

prey an animal hunted or killed by a predator for food.

savanna a grassy plain with few or no trees.

scavenge when animals eat dead animals that they did not kill themselves.

survive to continue to live or exist.

Web Sites

To learn more about lions, visit ABDO Publishing Company online. Web sites about lions are featured on our Book Links page. These links are routinely monitored and updated to provide the most current information available.

www.abdopublishing.com

Index

Africa **4, 5, 6, 8, 9, 28**

Asia **6**

body **10, 12, 15, 20, 21, 23, 25**

cheetahs **22**

communication **15, 16, 30**

cubs **14, 22, 24, 25, 26, 27, 30**

dangers **24, 28**

eating habits **20, 22, 23, 26**

elephants **9**

Europe **6**

fighting **10, 18**

fur and hair **10, 11, 12**

habitat **6, 28**

hunting **7, 16, 20, 22, 23, 26**

hyenas **22, 24**

India **5, 6, 28**

leopards **9, 24**

mammals **24**

mane **10, 11**

prides **14, 15, 16, 17, 18, 19, 22, 24, 26**

rhinoceroses **9, 20**

Sahara Desert **8**

size **12, 13, 24**

Swahili **8**

tigers **12, 13, 30**

United States **8, 9**

weather **5, 17**